Quotable
Shakespeare

QUOTABLE SHAKESPEARE

Summersdale Publishers Ltd
46 West Street
Chichester
West Sussex
PO19 1RP
UK

www.summersdale.com

Printed and bound in the Czech Republic

ISBN: 978-1-84953-584-7

Substantial discounts on bulk quantities of Summersdale books are available to corporations, professional associations and other organisations. For details contact Nicky Douglas by telephone: +44 (0) 1243 756902, fax: +44 (0) 1243 786300 or email: nicky@summersdale.com.

Quotable

Shakespeare

summersdale

Contents

Love's Labour

*This is the third man
that e'er I saw; the first
That e'er I sigh'd for.*

Miranda, *The Tempest*

Is love a tender thing?
it is too rough,
Too rude, too boisterous,
and it pricks like thorn.

Romeo, Romeo and Juliet

*Love comforteth like
sunshine after rain.*

'Venus and Adonis'

*Beauty itself doth of
itself persuade
The eyes of men
without an orator.*

'The Rape of Lucrece'

Some Cupid kills with arrows, some with traps.

Hero, *Much Ado About Nothing*

*The hind that would
be mated by the lion
Must die for love.*

Helena, *All's Well That Ends Well*

No sooner met but they looked; no sooner looked but they loved; no sooner loved but they sighed; no sooner sighed but they asked one another the reason.

Rosalind, *As You Like It*

*It gives me wonder great as
my content
To see you here before me.
O my soul's joy!
If after every tempest come
such calms,
May the winds blow till
they have waken'd death!*

Othello, *Othello*

*It is the show and seal
of nature's truth,
Where love's strong passion
is impress'd in youth.*

Countess of Rousillon, *All's Well That Ends Well*

This bud of love, by summer's ripening breath, May prove a beauteous flower when next we meet.

Juliet, *Romeo and Juliet*

Love looks not with the eyes, but with the mind, And therefore is wing'd Cupid painted blind.

Helena, *A Midsummer Night's Dream*

I, *beyond all limit of*
what else i' the world
Do love, prize, honour you.

Ferdinand, *The Tempest*

What power is it which mounts my love so high, That makes me see, and cannot feed mine eye?

Helena, *All's Well That Ends Well*

*But love is blind and
lovers cannot see
The pretty follies that
themselves commit.*

Jessica, *The Merchant of Venice*

*The course of true love
never did run smooth.*

Lysander, *A Midsummer Night's Dream*

Fate
and
Fortune

What fates impose, that men must needs abide; It boots not to resist both wind and tide.

King Edward, *Henry VI, Part 3*

*When Fortune means
to men most good,
She looks upon them
with a threatening eye.*

Cardinal Pandulf, *King John*

Mend your speech a little,
Lest it may mar
your fortunes.

King Lear, *King Lear*

If chance will have me king,
why, chance may crown me,
Without my stir.

Macbeth, *Macbeth*

If we are mark'd to die, we are enough To do our country loss; and if to live, The fewer men, the greater share of honour.

King Henry V, *Henry V*

Apollo's angry; and the heavens themselves Do strike at my injustice.

Leontes, *The Winter's Tale*

*O God! That one might
read the book of fate,
And see the revolution
of the times
Make mountains level,
and the continent,
Weary of solid firmness,
melt itself
Into the sea!*

King Henry IV, *Henry IV, Part 2*

Fortune brings in some boats that are not steer'd.

Pisanio, *Cymbeline*

*All the world's a stage,
And all the men and
women merely players:
They have their exits
and their entrances;
And one man in his time
plays many parts.*

Jaques, *As You Like It*

The stars above us,
govern our conditions.

Earl of Kent, *King Lear*

*Men at some time are
masters of their fates:
The fault, dear Brutus,
is not in our stars,
But in ourselves, that
we are underlings.*

Cassius, *Julius Caesar*

*Alack, our terrene moon
Is now eclipsed; and
it portends alone
The fall of Antony!*

Mark Antony, *Antony and Cleopatra*

*Let us sit and mock
the good housewife
Fortune from
her wheel, that her
gifts may henceforth
be bestowed equally.*

Celia, *As You Like It*

Our wills and fates
do so contrary run
That our devices still
are overthrown;
Our thoughts are ours, their
ends none of our own.

Player King, *Hamlet*

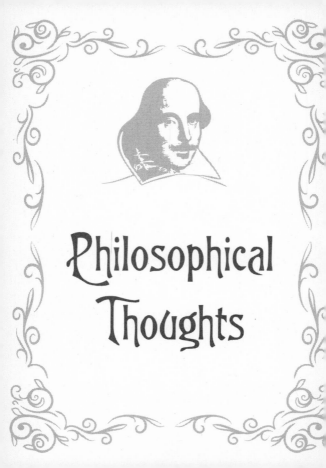

Philosophical Thoughts

Truth hath a quiet breast.

Thomas Mowbray, *Richard II*

We wound our modesty
and make foul the clearness
of our deservings,
When of ourselves
we publish them.

Steward, *All's Well That Ends Well*

*Why then, can one desire
too much of a good thing?*

Rosalind, *As You Like It*

Having nothing,
nothing can he lose.

Earl of Warwick, *Henry VI, Part 3*

*If to do were as easy as
to know what were good
to do, chapels had been
churches and poor men's
cottages princes' palaces.*

Portia, *The Merchant of Venice*

*The best wishes that can be
forged in your thoughts be
servants to you!*

Bertram, *All's Well That Ends Well*

What's in a name? That which we call a rose, By any other name would smell as sweet.

Juliet, *Romeo and Juliet*

Come what come may,
Time and the hour runs
through the roughest day.

Macbeth, *Macbeth*

Brevity is the soul of wit.

Polonius, *Hamlet*

Well, every one can master a grief but he that has it.

Benedick, *Much Ado About Nothing*

Courting
and
Marriage

*I know I am too mean
to be your queen,
And yet too good to
be your concubine.*

Lady Grey, Henry VI, Part 3

Sigh no more, ladies,
sigh no more,
Men were deceivers ever,
One foot in sea and
one on shore,
To one thing constant never.

Balthasar, *Much Ado About Nothing*

If there be no great love in the beginning, yet heaven may decrease it upon better acquaintance, when we are married and have more occasion to know one another; I hope, upon familiarity will grow more contempt.

Slender, *The Merry Wives of Windsor*

One half of me is yours,
the other half yours,
Mine own, I would say;
but if mine, then yours,
And so all yours.

Portia, *The Merchant of Venice*

Yet hasty marriage
seldom proveth well.

Richard, Duke of Gloucester, *Henry VI, Part 3*

*What's mine is yours and
what is yours is mine.*

Vincentio, *Measure for Measure*

*Was ever woman in this humour woo'd?
Was ever woman in this humour won?
I'll have her; but I will not keep her long.*

Richard, Duke of Gloucester, *Richard III*

*She's beautiful, and
therefore to be woo'd;
She is a woman,
therefore to be won.*

Earl of Suffolk, *Henry VI, Part I*

*Get thee a good husband,
and use him as he uses thee.*

Parolles, *All's Well That Ends Well*

Many a good hanging prevents a bad marriage.

Feste, *Twelfth Night*

That man that hath a tongue, I say, is no man, If with his tongue he cannot win a woman.

Valentine, *The Two Gentlemen of Verona*

*Marriage is a matter
of more worth
Than to be dealt in
by attorneyship.*

Earl of Suffolk, *Henry VI, Part I*

*I gyve unto my wief
my second best bed
with the furniture.*

From Shakespeare's will

The
Balance
of Power

*Uneasy lies the head
that wears a crown.*

King Henry IV, *Henry IV, Part 2*

O, it is excellent
To have a giant's strength;
but it is tyrannous
To use it like a giant.

Isabella, *Measure for Measure*

Where having nothing,
nothing can he lose.

Earl of Warwick, *Henry VI, Part 3*

Why, man, he doth bestride
the narrow world
Like a Colossus, and
we petty men
Walk under his huge
legs and peep about
To find ourselves
dishonourable graves.

Cassius, *Julius Caesar*

Faith, there had been many great men that have flattered the people, who ne'er loved them; and there be many that they have loved, they know not wherefore.

Second Officer, *Coriolanus*

Not all the water in
the rough rude sea
Can wash the balm off
from an anointed king;
The breath of worldly
men cannot depose
The deputy elected by the Lord.

King Richard II, *Richard II*

*Fearless minds climb
soonest unto crowns.*

Richard, Duke of Gloucester, *Henry VI, Part 3*

I would not be a queen
For all the world.

Anne Bullen, *Henry VIII*

I'll never
Be such a gosling to obey
instinct, but stand,
As if a man were
author of himself
And knew no other kin.

Coriolanus, *Coriolanus*

*Authority melts from me:
of late, when I cried 'Ho!'
Like boys unto a muss,
kings would start forth,
And cry 'Your will?' Have
you no ears? I am
Antony yet.*

Mark Antony, *Antony and Cleopatra*

No *ceremony that to*
great ones 'longs,
Not the king's crown, nor
the deputed sword,
The marshal's truncheon,
nor the judge's robe,
Become them with one
half so good a grace
As mercy does.

Isabella, *Measure for Measure*

I am greater than a king:
For when I was a
king, my flatterers
Were then but subjects;
being now a subject,
I have a king here
to my flatterer.
Being so great, I have
no need to beg.

King Richard II, *Richard II*

Every subject's duty is the king's; but every subject's soul is his own.

Henry V, *Henry V*

*Some are born great,
some achieve greatness,
and some have greatness
thrust upon them.*

Malvolio, *Twelfth Night*

This Mortal Coil

*Like as the waves make
towards the pebbled shore,
So do our minutes
hasten to their end.*

Sonnet 60

*The setting sun, and
music at the close,
As the last taste of
sweets, is sweetest last,
Writ in remembrance more
than things long past.*

John of Gaunt, *Richard II*

*I would that I were
low laid in my grave:
I am not worth this coil
that's made for me.*

Arthur, *King John*

Give me my robe, put on my crown; I have Immortal longings in me.

Cleopatra, *Antony and Cleopatra*

Duncan is in his grave;
After life's fitful fever
he sleeps well;
Treason has done his worst.

Macbeth, Macbeth

The minutes how they run,
How many make the
hour full complete;
How many hours bring
about the day;
How many days will
finish up the year;
How many years a
mortal man may live.

King Henry VI, *Henry VI, Part 3*

*Then began the tempest
to my soul,
Who pass'd, methought,
the melancholy flood,
With that grim ferryman
which poets write of,
Unto the kingdom of
perpetual night.*

Clarence, *Richard III*

*Ask for me to-morrow,
and you shall find
me a grave man.*

Mercutio, *Romeo and Juliet*

We are such stuff
As dreams are made
on, and our little life
Is rounded with a sleep.

Prospero, *The Tempest*

Tell me what blessings
I have here alive,
That I should fear to die?

Hermione, *The Winter's Tale*

Thou know'st 'tis common;
all that lives must die,
Passing through
nature to eternity.

Queen Gertrude, *Hamlet*

*Golden lads and
girls all must,
As chimney-sweepers,
come to dust.*

Guiderius, *Cymbeline*

We cannot hold
mortality's strong hand.

King John, *King John*

*Why, he that cuts off
twenty years of life
Cuts off so many years
of fearing death.*

Cassius, *Julius Caesar*

*The ripest fruit first
falls, and so doth he;
His time is spent, our
pilgrimage must be.*

King Richard II, *Richard II*

Men must endure
Their going hence, even
as their coming hither;
Ripeness is all: come on.

Edgar, *King Lear*

*Forbear to judge, for
we are sinners all.
Close up his eyes and
draw the curtain close;
And let us all to meditation.*

King Henry VI, *Henry VI, Part 2*

To die, to sleep;
To sleep: perchance
to dream.

Hamlet, *Hamlet*

If you prick us, do we not bleed? If you tickle us, do we not laugh? If you poison us, do we not die? And if you wrong us, shall we not revenge?

Shylock, *The Merchant of Venice*

*Good frend for Jesus
sake forbeare,
To digg the dust
encloased heare.
Blese be the man that
spares thes stones,
And curst be he that
moves my bones.*

Shakespeare's epitaph

Good
and
Evil

To win me soon to hell,
my female evil
Tempteth my better
angel from my side,
And would corrupt my
saint to be a devil,
Wooing his purity with
her foul pride

Sonnet 144

*Thy overflow of good
converts to bad,
And thy abundant
goodness shall excuse
This deadly blot in
thy digressing son.*

Henry Bolingbroke, *Richard II*

I am a man
More sinn'd against
than sinning.

King Lear, *King Lear*

*How oft the sight of
means to do ill deeds
Make deeds ill done!*

King John, *King John*

Some rise by sin, and some by virtue fall.

Escalus, *Measure for Measure*

Stars, hide your fires;
Let not light see my
black and deep desires.

Macbeth, *Macbeth*

Villain, thou know'st no law of God nor man: No beast so fierce but knows some touch of pity.

Lady Anne, *Richard III*

Where be these enemies?
Capulet! Montague!
See, what a scourge is
laid upon your hate,
That heaven finds means to
kill your joys with love!

Prince Escalus, *Romeo and Juliet*

*Men's evil manners live
in brass; their virtues
We write in water.*

Griffith, *Henry VIII*

What we changed
Was innocence for
innocence; we knew not
The doctrine of ill-
doing, nor dream'd
That any did.

Polixenes, *The Winter's Tale*

What a piece of work is a man! how noble in reason! [...]
And yet, to me, what is this quintessence of dust? man delights not me: no, nor woman neither, though by your smiling you seem to say so.

Hamlet, *Hamlet*

To beguile the time,
Look like the time; bear
welcome in your eye,
Your hand, your tongue: look
like the innocent flower,
But be the serpent under 't.

Lady Macbeth, *Macbeth*

*The evil that men do
lives after them;
The good is oft interred
with their bones.*

Mark Antony, *Julius Caesar*

*But I am in
So far in blood that sin
will pluck on sin:
Tear-falling pity dwells
not in this eye.*

King Richard III, *Richard III*

O, wonder!
How many goodly
creatures are there here!
How beauteous mankind
is! O brave new world,
That has such people in 't!

Miranda, *The Tempest*

There's no trust,
No faith, no honesty
in men; all perjured,
All forsworn, all naught,
all dissemblers.

Nurse, *Romeo and Juliet*

When we for recompense
have prais'd the vile,
It stains the glory in
that happy verse
Which aptly sings the good.

Poet, *Timon of Athens*

There is nothing either good or bad, but thinking makes it so.

Hamlet, *Hamlet*

*And therefore, since I
cannot prove a lover,
To entertain these fair
well-spoken days,
I am determined to
prove a villain
And hate the idle pleasures
of these days.*

Richard, *Duke of Gloucester, Richard III*

Sound
and
Fury

*York lies; he might have
sent and had the horse;
I owe him little duty,
and less love;
And take foul scorn to
fawn on him by sending.*

Duke of Somerset, *Henry VI, Part 1*

And all the gods go with
you! upon your sword
Sit laurel victory! and
smooth success
Be strew'd before your feet!

Cleopatra, *Antony and Cleopatra*

As he was valiant, I honour him: but, as he was ambitious, I slew him.

Brutus, *Julius Caesar*

*A pox o' your throat, you
bawling, blasphemous,
incharitable dog!*

Sebastian, *The Tempest*

I pray thee, good
Mercutio, let's retire:
The day is hot, the
Capulets abroad,
And, if we meet, we shall
not scape a brawl;
For now, these hot days, is
the mad blood stirring.

Benvolio, Romeo and Juliet

*Please ye we may contrive
this afternoon,
And quaff carouses to
our mistress' health,
And do as adversaries do in law,
Strive mightily, but eat
and drink as friends.*

Tranio, *The Taming of the Shrew*

Come not between the dragon and his wrath.

King Lear, *King Lear*

Let there be gall enough in thy ink; though thou write with a goose-pen, no matter.

Sir Toby Belch, *Twelfth Night*

*Give back, or else
embrace thy death;
Come not within the
measure of my wrath.*

Valentine, *The Two Gentlemen of Verona*

Though with their high wrongs
I am struck to the quick,
Yet with my nobler
reason 'gainst my fury
Do I take part: the
rarer action is
In virtue than in vengeance.

Prospero, *The Tempest*

What, drawn, and talk of peace! I hate the word, As I hate hell, all Montagues, and thee.

Tybalt, *Romeo and Juliet*

*Sir, you have wrestled
well and overthrown
More than your enemies.*

Rosalind, *As You Like It*

*As wicked dew as e'er
my mother brush'd
With raven's feather
from unwholesome fen
Drop on you both! A
south-west blow on ye
And blister you all o'er!*

Caliban, *The Tempest*

Get thee back to Caesar,
Tell him thy entertainment:
look, thou say
He makes me angry with
him; for he seems
Proud and disdainful,
harping on what I am,
Not what he knew I was:
he makes me angry.

Mark Antony, Antony and Cleopatra

Let me have war, say I;
it exceeds peace as far as
day does night; it's spritely,
waking, audible, and
full of vent.

First Servant, *Coriolanus*

Old Age

*My glass shall not
persuade me I am old,
So long as youth and
thou are of one date.*

Sonnet 22

I wasted time, and now doth time waste me.

King Richard II, *Richard II*

Beauty doth varnish age, as if new-born, And gives the crutch the cradle's infancy: O, 'tis the sun that maketh all things shine.

Biron, *Love's Labour's Lost*

But age, with his
stealing steps,
Hath claw'd me
in his clutch,
And hath shipped
me intil the land,
As if I had never been such.

Clown, *Hamlet*

And wherefore say not
I that I am old?
O, love's best habit is
in seeming trust,
And age in love loves
not to have years told.

Sonnet 138

*Nay, sit, nay, sit, good
cousin Capulet;
For you and I are past
our dancing days.*

Capulet, *Romeo and Juliet*

I would there were no age between sixteen and three-and-twenty, or that youth would sleep out the rest; for there is nothing in the between but getting wenches with child, wronging the ancientry, stealing, fighting – Hark you now!

Shepherd, *The Winter's Tale*

Your lordship, though not clean past your youth, hath yet some smack of age in you, some relish of the saltness of time; and I must humbly beseech your lordship to have a reverent care of your health.

Falstaff, *Henry IV, Part 2*

*Doth not the appetite
alter? A man loves the
meat in his youth that he
cannot endure in his age.*

Benedick, *Much Ado About Nothing*

*Nothing 'gainst Time's
scythe can make defence
Save breed, to brave him
when he takes thee hence.*

Sonnet 12

*Though I look old, yet
I am strong and lusty;
For in my youth I
never did apply
Hot and rebellious
liquors in my blood.*

Adam, *As You Like It*

So wise so young, they say, do never live long.

Richard, Duke of Gloucester, *Richard III*

The
Food
of Love

Give me some music;
music, moody food
Of us that trade in love.

Cleopatra, *Antony and Cleopatra*

For Orpheus' lute was strung with poets' sinews, Whose golden touch could soften steel and stones, Make tigers tame and huge leviathans Forsake unsounded deeps to dance on sands.

Proteus, *The Two Gentlemen of Verona*

*The man that hath no
music in himself,
Nor is not moved with
concord of sweet sounds,
Is fit for treasons,
stratagems and spoils.*

Lorenzo, *The Merchant of Venice*

*Play, music! And you, brides
and bridegrooms all,
With measure heap'd in
joy, to the measures fall.*

Duke Senior, *As You Like It*

'Tis good; though music
oft hath such a charm
To make bad good, and
good provoke to harm.

Vincentio, *Measure for Measure*

Orpheus with his
lute made trees,
And the mountain
tops that freeze,
Bow themselves when
he did sing:
To his music plants and flowers
Ever sprung; as sun and showers
There had made a lasting spring.

Henry VIII

*How sweet the moonlight
sleeps upon this bank!
Here will we sit and let
the sounds of music
Creep in our ears: soft
stillness and the night
Become the touches of
sweet harmony.*

Lorenzo, *The Merchant of Venice*

Most heavenly music!
It nips me unto listening,
and thick slumber
Hangs upon mine eyes.

Pericles, Pericles, Prince of Tyre

O, *musicians, because
my heart itself plays* 'My
heart is full of woe': O,
*play me some merry
dump, to comfort me.*

Peter, *Romeo and Juliet*

Go, Philostrate,
Stir up the Athenian
youth to merriments;
Awake the pert and
nimble spirit of mirth.

Theseus, A Midsummer Night's Dream

*If music be the food
of love, play on.*

Duke Orsino, *Twelfth Night*

If you're interested in finding out more about our books, find us on Facebook at Summersdale Publishers and follow us on Twitter at @Summersdale.

www.summersdale.com